Dear Santa,

CHRISTMAS Photos

CHRISTMAS DAY *Planner*

Morning

Afternoon

Evening

CHRISTMAS DAY *Memories*

My Favorite Memory	Highlight of the Day

CHRISTMAS WISH List

WHAT I'M HOPING FOR

THINGS I REALLY NEED

MY FAVORITE THINGS

CHRISTMAS *Journal*

CHRISTMAS Countdown

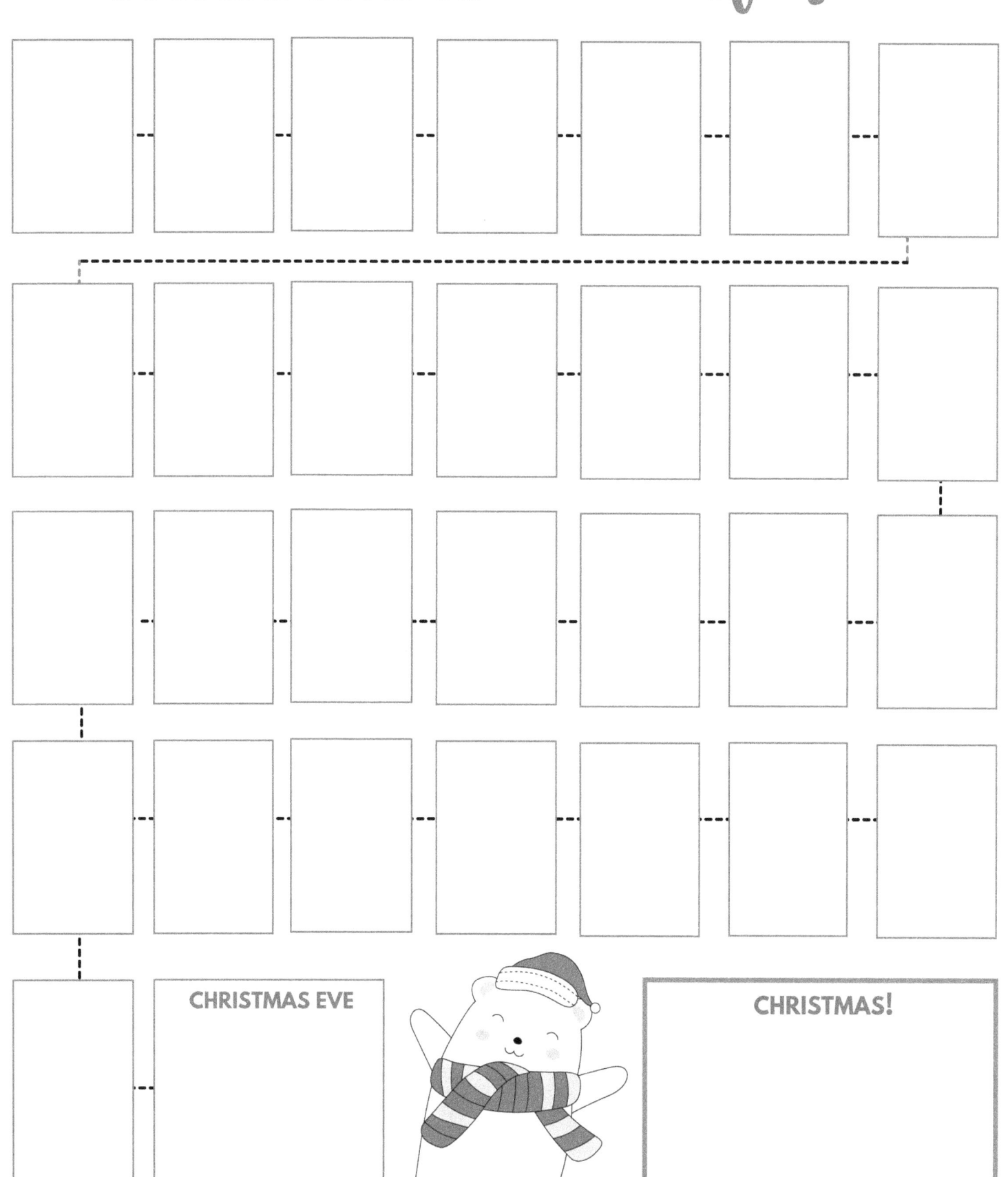

CHRISTMAS EVE

CHRISTMAS!

CHRISTMAS Journal

ONLINE SHOPPING *Tracker*

ITEM	WEBSITE	COST	RECEIVED?

NOTES & REMINDERS

CHRISTMAS *Journal*

CHRISTMAS SUPPLY List

CHRISTMAS GIFT *Ideas*

NAME: _____   **BUDGET:** _____

GIFT IDEAS

NAME: _____   **BUDGET:** _____

GIFT IDEAS

NAME: _____   **BUDGET:** _____

GIFT IDEAS

NAME: _____   **BUDGET:** _____

GIFT IDEAS

NOTES

CHRISTMAS PARTY *Planner*

LOCATION		DATE	

THEME	DRESS CODE	NOTES

SCHEDULE

TO DO LIST

ACTIVITIES / IDEAS

MEAL PLANNER

HOLIDAY WEEK *Schedule*

MON	
TUE	
WED	
THU	
FRI	
SAT	
SUN	

PRIORITIES

TO DO

NOTES

Décor PLANNER

THEME

BUDGET

ACTUAL COST

IDEAS

SCHEDULE

COLOR SCHEME

THINGS TO BUY

NOTES

CHRISTMAS SHOPPING *List*

ITEM   PRICE   STORE

NOTES & REMINDERS

CHRISTMAS GIFT Tracker

NAME	GIFT	BOUGHT

CHRISTMAS CARD *Tracker*

RECIPIENT:
ADDRESS:

○ WRITTEN　　○ MAILED　　○ RECEIVED

RECIPIENT:
ADDRESS:

○ WRITTEN　　○ MAILED　　○ RECEIVED

RECIPIENT:
ADDRESS:

○ WRITTEN　　○ MAILED　　○ RECEIVED

RECIPIENT:
ADDRESS:

○ WRITTEN　　○ MAILED　　○ RECEIVED

RECIPIENT:
ADDRESS:

○ WRITTEN　　○ MAILED　　○ RECEIVED

CHRISTMAS PARTY *Invites*

NAME	CONTACT INFORMATION	RSVP'D

CHRISTMAS BUDGET *Tracker*

TOTAL BUDGET GOAL

ACTUAL COST

NAME	BUDGET	GIFT PURCHASED	AMOUNT SPENT

CHRISTMAS GIFT Tracker

NAME OF STORE	ITEM TO PURCHASE	COST

ELF ON THE SHELF *Ideas*

SUPPLY LIST

OTHER IDEAS

 # CHRISTMAS COOKIE *Recipe*

RECIPE NAME:

Category: **Source:** **Prep Time:**

Temperature: **Cook Time:** **Serves:**

INGREDIENTS

DIRECTIONS

NOTES

HOLIDAY *Recipes*

SERVES: **PREP TIME:** **BAKE TIME:**

Ingredients

- [ ]
- [ ]
- [ ]
- [ ]
- [ ]
- [ ]
- [ ]
- [ ]
- [ ]
- [ ]

Instructions

CHRISTMAS Journal

CHRISTMAS Journal

Dear Santa,

CHRISTMAS *Photos*

CHRISTMAS DAY *Planner*

Morning

Afternoon

Evening

CHRISTMAS DAY *Memories*

| My Favorite Memory | Highlight of the Day |
|---|---|//

CHRISTMAS WISH List

WHAT I'M HOPING FOR

THINGS I REALLY NEED

MY FAVORITE THINGS

CHRISTMAS Journal

CHRISTMAS Countdown

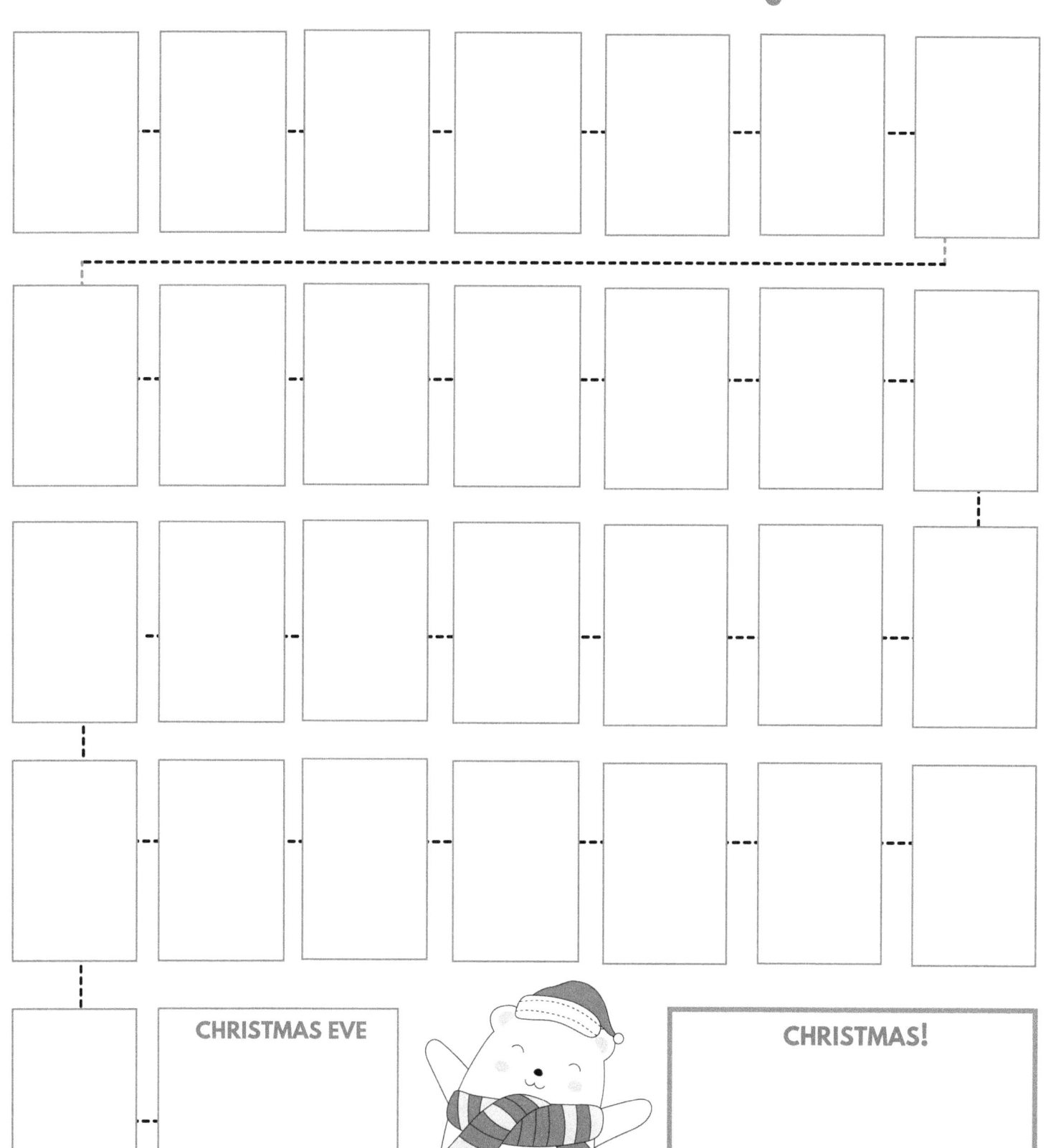

CHRISTMAS EVE

CHRISTMAS!

CHRISTMAS Journal

ONLINE SHOPPING *Tracker*

ITEM	WEBSITE	COST	RECEIVED?

NOTES & REMINDERS

CHRISTMAS *Journal*

CHRISTMAS SUPPLY *List*

CHRISTMAS GIFT *Ideas*

NAME: BUDGET:

GIFT IDEAS

NAME: BUDGET:

GIFT IDEAS

NAME: BUDGET:

GIFT IDEAS

NAME: BUDGET:

GIFT IDEAS

NOTES

CHRISTMAS PARTY *Planner*

LOCATION		DATE	

THEME	DRESS CODE	NOTES

SCHEDULE

TO DO LIST

ACTIVITIES / IDEAS

MEAL PLANNER

HOLIDAY WEEK *Schedule*

Day	
MON	
TUE	
WED	
THU	
FRI	
SAT	
SUN	

PRIORITIES

TO DO

NOTES

Décor PLANNER

THEME

BUDGET

ACTUAL COST

IDEAS

SCHEDULE

COLOR SCHEME

THINGS TO BUY

NOTES

CHRISTMAS SHOPPING *List*

ITEM	PRICE	STORE

NOTES & REMINDERS

CHRISTMAS GIFT *Tracker*

NAME	GIFT	BOUGHT

CHRISTMAS CARD *Tracker*

RECIPIENT:
ADDRESS:

○ WRITTEN ○ MAILED ○ RECEIVED

RECIPIENT:
ADDRESS:

○ WRITTEN ○ MAILED ○ RECEIVED

RECIPIENT:
ADDRESS:

○ WRITTEN ○ MAILED ○ RECEIVED

RECIPIENT:
ADDRESS:

○ WRITTEN ○ MAILED ○ RECEIVED

RECIPIENT:
ADDRESS:

○ WRITTEN ○ MAILED ○ RECEIVED

CHRISTMAS PARTY *Invites*

NAME	CONTACT INFORMATION	RSVP'D

CHRISTMAS BUDGET *Tracker*

TOTAL BUDGET GOAL	ACTUAL COST

NAME	BUDGET	GIFT PURCHASED	AMOUNT SPENT

CHRISTMAS GIFT *Tracker*

NAME OF STORE	ITEM TO PURCHASE	COST

ELF ON THE SHELF *Ideas*

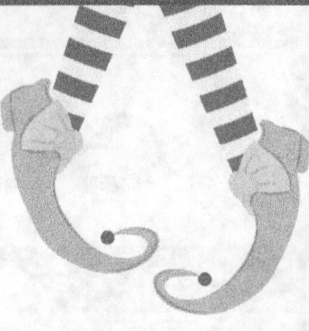

SUPPLY LIST

OTHER IDEAS

 # CHRISTMAS COOKIE Recipe

RECIPE NAME:

Category: **Source:** **Prep Time:**

Temperature: **Cook Time:** **Serves:**

INGREDIENTS

DIRECTIONS

NOTES

HOLIDAY *Recipes*

SERVES: **PREP TIME:** **BAKE TIME:**

Ingredients

Instructions

CHRISTMAS Journal

CHRISTMAS Journal

www.ingramcontent.com/pod-product-compliance
Lightning Source LLC
Chambersburg PA
CBHW081159070526
44583CB00021B/2906